GONE
TO THE
DAWGS

Robert Mason

CONTENTS

Print ISBN: 978-1-09833-903-6
eBook ISBN: 978-1-09833-904-3

INTRODUCTION

This book is dedicated to all the first responders who hold the Thin Blue Line between good and evil, keeping the rest of us safe as we go about our daily lives. I am proud to say that I served the City of Houston Police Department for thirty-five years and ten months. The first nineteen years I was assigned to the Central Patrol Division where I was a Field Training Officer ("FTO") and assigned to the SWAT Perimeter Team. The last seventeen years of my career were spent in the K-9 detail. During my job assignment working as a K-9 handler I learned more about dogs than you could ever imagine. There is an old saying that if you love your job, you never have to work a day in your life. I had the best job in the world, and while assigned to the K-9 detail got paid to pet a dog!

When I first started working in the K-9 detail, I was told that my dog was considered a piece of equipment and expendable to save my life or the life of another police officer, if necessary, in the line of duty. What they do not tell you is this animal would become the most trusted partner I would ever have and become a part of my family. I have always heard a dog is the only animal on the planet who will love you more than he loves himself. These animals are worth their weight in gold and every penny spent on them. The police canines have saved countless lives of police officers across the country and at times have been injured or killed in the process.

All the dogs in the K-9 detail come from overseas. Local canine vendors here in the United States will travel to countries like Germany, France, Hungary, and the Czech Republic to seek out the top dogs that are bred from excellent bloodlines for either Military and/or Law Enforcement application. These dogs begin their training early on as young pups in obedience, agility, tracking, bite work, drug detection, and bomb detection. The local vendors make their selections after viewing the dogs while they are being trained overseas and upon purchasing them the dogs are shipped back to the United States to continue their training here. The police departments usually will contact the local canine vendors prior to visiting them and will request to see specific types of dogs they are looking for, such as German Shepherds, Dutch Shepherds, and/or Belgian Malinois. At the end of their training the dogs will become either a single purpose patrol dog, a dual-purpose patrol (drug) dog, and/or a dual-purpose patrol (bomb) dog. Police departments pay "large sums of money" for these dogs, which usually run between nine-thousand and sixteen-thousand dollars for each dog depending on their age, sex, title, pedigree, and level of training. The police department pays for the specialized equipment that is required for each K-9 vehicle such as the large insert cages needed for the dogs, remote controlled pop out doors, and temperature controlled heat sensors that are activated if the vehicle accidentally turns off or the air conditioner stops working. The police departments also pay for all veterinarian care and food for each dog.

The K-9 dog handlers selected for the police K-9 detail are usually "green" dog handlers, meaning that none of them have hardly any dog training experience. It is better this way because the police department trainers avoid wasting time butting heads with the new dog handler regarding the best way to train the canine. A lot of times during the sixteen-week basic K-9 handler school it is the "rookie" dog handler himself that needs more training than the dog. Even with highly trained police canines, at the end of the day they are still dogs and will at times resort back to doing the silly things that regular untrained dogs do!

To all the men and women who have ever held the dumb end of a leash in their hands and followed behind a four-legged fur missile, I tip my hat to you! Only one percent of police officers become K-9 handlers. It is one of the most dangerous jobs in the department. I was lucky to have the opportunity to work with three excellent police dogs. We always looked out for each other. I sincerely hope we made a difference with all the arrests that we made and helped remove a few of the many bad guys that were running the streets. As insignificant as each individual criminal arrest seems, I can only hope that we kept the city a little bit safer for the folks who live there and let them sleep better at night. As the saying goes, when citizens need help, they call the police, and when the police need help, they call K-9.

I would like to thank my wife of thirty-one plus years Robyn Mason, and my two grown children (Carrie and Cody) who have supported me throughout my career. They have sacrificed countless hours at home all alone having to do for themselves while I was out protecting others working my regular shift, working overtime, and/or working extra jobs. Without their love and support, my everyday life would not be complete!

This book contains interesting police stories that I encountered either myself or was told about by other police officers while working in the Patrol Division and the K-9 Detail during the span of my entire career with the Houston Police Department. I would like to thank all the many police officers that I have had the privilege to work with over the years running all these crazy calls together and keeping each other safe. You will always be in my thoughts and prayers for the rest of my life. Your friend always, Unit#73K31 signing off!

> *"The wicked flee though no one pursues, but the righteous are as bold as a lion." (Proverbs 28:1) (NIV)*

> *"Blessed are the peacemakers, for they shall be called children of God." (Matthew 5:9) (KJV)*

> *Courage is not the absence of fear, but the capacity to act despite our fears. (John McCain)*

GONE TO THE DAWGS

1. THE POLITE DRUNK DRIVER

While on routine patrol one night, I see this car weaving all over the road and attempt to stop the vehicle, but the guy does not stop. I activate my emergency equipment and continue to follow him for several miles until he finally exits the freeway and stops. I approach the male driver who appears extremely intoxicated and ask him why he did not stop sooner. The driver replies, "Sorry officer. I thought you were trying to stop the car behind me." I reply by saying, "I was the car behind you!"

2. DO-NUT SHOP BURGLAR

Police officers get dispatched to a burglary in-progress call at a local Shipley Do-Nut Shop and several cops show up very quickly. Looking inside through the glass they see the suspect still inside the location and call for a police canine. Upon arrival to the scene the K-9 team goes inside and locates the suspect who is hiding behind the front counter. The canine engages the suspect who grabs the dog around the neck with his hands, arm's length away from his body. The suspect yells out loud, "I know about these canines," and continues holding the dog at bay from biting him. The K-9 handler walks up to the suspect and asks him, "Do you know about SL-20 flashlights?" The handler then assists his canine partner and makes sure he wins the battle. The suspect is taken into custody and the incident is over without any injuries to the police officers involved. I hope the suspect will think twice before breaking into a donut shop (cops favorite) and playing hide and seek with a highly trained police canine.

3. LADY IN THE WRONG HOUSE

I was dispatched to a burglary-in-progress call where the owners were not at home and their alarm system was activated. Upon arrival we found a broken living room window on the front side of the home and waited for our back-up unit to arrive. While we were waiting, the front door swings open and this lady who is wearing a night gown steps outside to greet us. She claims that she is the owner and that her alarm was activated by accident due to her entering an incorrect code. We asked her how the window was broken out and she stated it was from a previous break-in and that it had not yet been repaired. We asked her for some type of identification, and she told us that her wallet had been stolen along with all her information. She assured us that she lived there and even invited us inside the house showing us pictures of herself in miscellaneous picture frames on lamp stands and tables. While we are still there scratching our heads wondering how someone could have such bad luck, the "real" owners show-up and ask us who is the unknown lady that was wearing the owner's night gown? Come to find out this crazy lady had broken into the home and had brought her own family pictures with her to make it look as if she lived there.

4. BUTT NAKED

I received a burglary-in-progress call where upon arrival I was told by another officer that the suspect inside the location goes by the street name, "Butt Naked". I asked how he obtained this name and was told he had a tattoo on his chest that said, "Butt Naked". The suspect's motive was to break into a neighbor's home and remove all his clothes while fixing himself some lunch. At this point, I am not excited to enter the location but unfortunately had no choice. I along with other officers enter the location, attempting to be quiet, when we hear the T.V. on inside in the living room. I enter the room with my canine partner and see this big heavy dude sitting on the couch butt naked, watching T.V. and eating a bag of corn chips. I call out to him, "Police, get on the ground!" but he ignores me and continues eating. Officers run into the room and detain the large butt naked man, who appears surprised to see us there. Can you imagine coming home after a hard day's work to find "Butt Naked" making himself comfortable on your couch (naked), eating your food, or in your bathtub?

5. HIDE AND SEEK

Patrol officers were dispatched to a disturbance call where an ex-boyfriend was accused of assaulting his ex-girlfriend at her home. He attempts to run away on foot when the police arrive. The only problem is the suspect weighs approximately four hundred pounds. and he is seen jogging next door to hide in an unlocked two-story home that is under construction. He manages to run upstairs and pull down the ladder to the attic and climbs up them to hide. Police officers are hot on his trail and observe the suspect going into the attic area. They call out for him to stop, but he refuses to surrender. The officers set up a perimeter and call for a K-9 unit. This is where it begins to get a little crazy. Upon my arrival, the suspect has barricaded himself in a corner of the attic and placed his entire head underneath the attic insulation. Imagine a four hundred pound man attempting to conceal himself with only his head hidden by the attic insulation and the rest of his very large body exposed for all to see, like an ostrich hiding his head in the sand to avoid danger. This strategy did not work well for a man of his stature. Anyway, I go up into the hot attic with my canine partner and politely ask the man to surrender. After several attempts with no success, I had no choice but to send my canine to engage the suspect. The fight was on! He grabbed my dog by the head, and during the fight I heard the ceiling tile start to crack. The next thing I know I see the suspect falling through the ceiling. I begin pulling my dog's long leash back towards me as hard as I can to keep him safe from injury. The suspect crashes through the ceiling and lands on his feet like a cat. Unfortunately for him he landed between four or five officers who have been watching this unfold in the upstairs bedroom. The officers who were there later told me that the suspect immediately went into a kung-fu stance upon landing, and then attempted to run into a nearby bathroom. His getaway plan did not work, and his newfound freedom was short-lived due to the police officers surrounding him as he was taken into custody.

6. JUST A LITTLE BIT

I was dispatched to an alarm call at a business where officers found forced entry and believed a possible suspect might still be inside. Upon arrival, I met with the primary unit on the scene. After giving me all the information, he requested to go inside the location along with my canine partner and myself. I hesitantly agreed to let him go along, but for safety, I told him to stay close by my side during the search. Once inside the dark building, we somehow become separated and my dog is working off leash. Using my flashlight, I saw the officer standing down the hallway approximately fifteen to twenty feet away from me. My dog starts running towards him. I called out to my canine partner just as he is reaching the officer's location, attempting to call him back to me. I then hear the officer yell out as if he is in pain and could see him grabbing his pants near his crotch area with both of his hands. I asked the officer if he was okay and if the dog had bitten him? He responded, "A little bit," and continued holding the front of his pants. I asked him again, "Did the dog bite you or not?" Again, he responded, "A little bit, but I'm okay." I asked him to show me his injury, but he refused and exited the building holding his crotch, leaving me alone to finish the search with my canine partner. I felt guilty regarding what happened to my fellow officer, but I did warn him to stay close by my side during the search to ensure his safety.

7. MOTORCYCLE CHASE

While working a K-9 shift, I overheard a high-speed motorcycle chase going on over the police radio. I hear the patrol officer involved in the chase say over the radio that he could not read the license plate on the bike. However, the suspect was wearing a t-shirt that said, "If you can read this the bitch fell off." The officer later found the guy, still wearing the same shirt, attempting to blend in at a local Harley-Davidson dealership. They arrested him on the showroom floor.

8. UNDERWEAR CAPER

Police canines are not to be messed with and have been trained to take down violent criminals, and to not lose the battle. But they still do the unexpected when you least expect it. For example, I was dispatched to a burglary-in-progress call and patrol officers were on scene holding the perimeter. Upon arrival, my canine was immediately sent into the location to search for the suspect(s) and the patrol officers have a front row seat watching the action through the front window of the residence. The canine goes immediately to a clothes basket on the floor and pulls out a pair of women's dirty underwear and parades them proudly around the room in his mouth for all to see. One of the patrol officers looks at me with a big grin on his face and asks me, "How did you teach him to do that?"

9. EDIBLE UNDIES

On another call, the same canine did something else unexpected on a call regarding an actor on the ground (suspect running from the police) who was attempting to hide underneath a house. Officers have the house surrounded, but the suspect will not come out and K-9 is called in to apprehend the wanted person. Upon our arrival, I give one final warning to the suspect who is attempting to hide from the police and then the canine is released underneath the home. The dead silence is broken by the suspect, who is wearing daisy-duke shorts, screaming bloody murder as the canine drags him by one of his legs out from underneath the house. I was told later by the transporting officer that while the suspect was handcuffed in the back seat of the police car, he tells the officer in a surprising manner, "My underwear is missing. The police canine ate it!!"

10. MANDATORY ROTATION

When I first joined the police department back in the early 1980s, it was standard procedure that after you got off probation, you were required to serve a mandatory rotation either in Jail division for six months and/or Dispatch division for one year. I was sent to dispatch. At the time, they were slowly replacing all the uniform police officers with civilians which was really to our advantage. This shortened the one-year sentence by a few months. One of the crazy things I remember about working up there is we had an old out of date belt drive system that was only used during an emergency, such as when the main computer system would go down for some reason. The belt drive system was the so called "back-up system". The way it was setup, whenever the computer system went down, the call takers would fill out a small three-by-five index card and place it on the belt drive system. If everything worked the way the system was designed, that little index card would make its way from the call takers/telephone center (located on a different floor) along the belt drive system (track) and work its way down to the police dispatchers floor where a very patient police dispatcher would sort out all the index cards on their console and start dispatching all the calls out as quickly as possible by a priority code. The code system listed the seriousness of the call and the dispatchers would always dispatch the higher priority calls first (for instance, shootings and any type of in-progress call).

Sounds easy, right? Well, I wish I could say it worked as designed every time we used it, but it never did!! That dang belt drive system would always mess up and get jammed from all the little index cards getting smashed together on the belt drive. This would cause a massive malfunction (back-up) and none of the index cards were making it to their assigned destination. So, imagine sitting at a dispatch console staring at a blank screen for twenty to thirty minutes or longer waiting for something to drop at your console and all of a sudden someone breaks the dead silence by screaming from the back of the room that our belt drive system had been jammed up (not working) with hundreds of miscellaneous three-by-five cards. One moment you were almost falling asleep from pure boredom, and now you were in panic mode advising units over the police radio to stand-by for multiple calls to be dispatched. We would usually do this as quickly as possible by a general broadcast ("G.B.") and the patrol units would volunteer for the calls as we G.B. them one at a time over the radio. Fun memories no doubt!

11. THINGS YOU SHOULD NOT SAY TO A COP

Here are examples of "Things you should not say to a cop when you get pulled over." I stopped a man one time who had a box of donuts sitting in the passenger seat of his car. I said good morning and asked him for his driver's license. He seems to be in a bad mood as he hands over his license and says, "Do you want a donut, I know you cops love donuts?" At that point, there was not enough ink in my pen to write him for every violation permissible!

Another time, I was running radar where the speed limit was thirty-five mph. I clock this guy driving a Corvette going eighty-five mph. I pull him over and tell him he was driving 85/35 mph. He responds by saying, "Oh that couldn't have been me officer, because I was going much faster than that!"

12. RELATIVE ON A RIDE-ALONG

Long ago, you could take a friend or relative out through a ride-along program. I thought it would be a great idea to take my dad once on a little adventure. I was working evening shift at the time. It started out as a very normal day, stopping a few cars, and running some routine calls. During the shift, I volunteered to check out an alarm call at a business at about the same time my dad said he needed to use the restroom. I told him that I would check this call out quickly and then take him to use the restroom somewhere. Upon arrival to the call I quickly checked the perimeter of the building and observed no type of forced entry. I walked back to the police car where my dad was waiting patiently on me and I told him we were about to leave the location. I could now take him somewhere to use the restroom, but he looked at me and said, "Don't worry about it I took care of it already." I looked at him all confused and asked how did he do that? He responded by telling me that while I walked around the building, he got out of the marked patrol car and urinated in the parking lot next to my car. My face turned beet red as I glared across the street from where we were parked and observed several citizens staring directly at us from inside a local restaurant, which had a large plate glass window. I could have wrung my dad's neck at that point. There was no telling how many people watched him urinate in plain view outside of my police car!

13.   OFFICER DOWN/ASSIST THE OFFICER

We had a few old timers who worked day shift and almost every day this particular senior police officer would park his marked patrol car next to a busy street as if he were monitoring traffic, put on his police hat, nod his head and fall asleep. Well, it did not take long before citizens saw him out there and immediately start calling 9-1-1 to report an officer down (assist the officer). Everybody on the shift knew exactly who it was and where to find him. Usually the day shift patrol Sgt. would be assigned to go by the location and wake up the old timer, as this became a regular occurrence.

14.   BLACK BART

Back in the 1980s, they gave the old school salty police veterans the task of station security. Their job was to keep employees safe at the Central Police Station. They were also in charge of enforcing illegal parking around the station and would even write marked police cars tickets. The job given to these guys was not the most popular on the force due to the very nature of what they were doing, writing tickets, or towing cars of fellow police officers. If you got caught with a ticket on your windshield, you were bound to have a bad day, as you would be forced to report to the desk sergeant for a real ass chewing and possibly may be required to write a letter. The police officers who were given these types of assignments were very thick skinned and nobody would mess with them due to the police culture at the time. As a rookie officer, I avoided these guys like the plague as much as possible and did not want to make eye contact with them or interact with them for any reason. A lot of police officers would come to their attention while running late to work. They would park illegally in a fire lane or double park outside the station. One military style desk sergeant we had was made from the same fabric. If you arrived at work a few minutes late, he would attempt to make your life miserable. "Black Bart," who got his nickname from dressing all in black whenever he was not in uniform and off duty, would get right in your face (nose to nose) like a Marine drill sergeant and say, "Why were you late?" Unless you had a death in the family, or some other unforeseeable tragic accident like accidentally sawing your arm off, he was going to write you up! I do not think he liked me very much after he questioned me for being late once. I told him I was downstairs relieving myself. His face turned beet red and I thought his head was going to explode right there in roll call.

15. I THOUGHT YOU WERE DEAD

They told us in the police academy to always be aware of our surroundings, and I found out why. It was a slow day and I was parked underneath an overpass, hand-writing a report (this was before MDT computers), minding my own business. I left my driver's side window cracked open about four inches. I had only been there for approximately twenty minutes. Suddenly, I had this funny feeling that someone was watching me. I looked up and there was this homeless woman covered in dirt, with crazy hair, and gnats flying all around her face. She had her nose pushed up against my driver side window. As soon as we made eye contact, she started screaming at the top of her lungs and I started screaming back at her, probably just as loud, because she scared the crap out of me! I tell her to calm down over and over so she can tell me what is wrong? She finely catches her breath and says, "I thought you were dead because you weren't moving!" Oh boy, she almost made me poop in my pants!

16. MECHANIC BLOOPERS

Every three thousand miles (or whenever a problem occurred with our vehicle), officers are required to take their police cars to the city garage for maintenance. Usually all goes well, and we are back on the road fighting crime in no time. However, sometimes things do not go so well, and we must live with the consequences. One time, a mechanic forgot to put the oil back into a police car he was working on during the scheduled oil change and ruined the entire engine. Or the time a mechanic forgot to put all the lug nuts back on the wheels of a police car after a simple tire rotation. An officer picked up his car and made it about two blocks before all the wheels fell right off! Ask any officer that has been on the Department any amount of time and I am sure he will have plenty of stories like these. Over the years, I almost filled up my toolbox with the number of miscellaneous tools and flashlights I have found abandoned under the hood of my police car after some type of maintenance was completed.

17. THE CONFUSED POLICE CHIEF

It is funny watching people react when they see a police car driving up behind them with emergency equipment activated. They do not have a clue where they should go or what they should do. I have had people panic and stop in the middle of a moving lane on the freeway, and I think to myself, "Where did you get your driver's license?" The best one I can remember is when I was running a priority one call leaving the central police station. I got stuck driving behind our Chief of Police at the time who was driving on the freeway. Surprisingly, he was driving himself (most Chiefs have drivers) in an unmarked police car. I drove up behind him using my emergency equipment. He refused to pull over or get out of my way. I could see him staring at me in his rearview mirror. He acknowledges me by waving his hands like I was just doing it for fun since he was the "New Chief". After about two to three minutes of getting nowhere, I finally had to change lanes and drive around him since he refused to get out of the way of the emergency vehicle.

18. K-9 DOG CATCHER

I guess some people do not realize that you are the police even when you are in uniform and driving a marked K-9 police car. I received a hold-up alarm at a Burger King restaurant and pulled into the parking lot. As I exit from my car, an elderly lady parks right next to me. My police canine is going crazy barking at her and shaking the car. She has a British accent and she began asking me questions about the dog. "Is he mean?" "Is he vicious?" "Does he bite?" And then she finally asks, "What did he do?" In that moment I realized she thought I was a dog catcher instead of a K-9 police officer.

19. FUNNY NAMES

You meet all kinds of people working this type of job and some of them have got funny names. There was a panic alarm activated at a local "mom and pop" store. I get the call and upon arrival walk inside to speak to the person working behind the counter. She is a young lady named "Dam Hoe". I later advise the police dispatcher over the two-way radio that the alarm was accidently set off by "Dam Hoe."

20. LITTLE UPSET TUMMY

One of my former co-workers who worked in the K-9 detail was afraid of dogs. That is like saying you work in the Helicopter detail, but you are afraid to fly. He used to tell people that K-9 was the best job in the world, except for the dog and then laugh about it. The police dog he worked with liked to chew on and eat baseballs. He was too afraid to take the baseball away from the dog while it was in the dog's mouth for fear of getting bit and would let the dog eat them. Well, it did not take long before his dog started having stomach issues and refused to eat his dog food anymore. He takes the dog to the city veterinarian to find out what is wrong with him. An x-ray is taken, and the veterinarian tells him that he needs to take his dog to a well-known veterinarian school in Texas for more testing and surgery. The bill for that little upset tummy ended up being around seven thousand dollars.

21. HELP, I'VE BEEN SHOT

"Help I've been shot, but do not tell anybody or I will get in trouble!" Sounds crazy right? Yes, I know of at least two different occasions where officers have been shot either by a co-worker accidentally with a stun gun/taser or have accidentally shot themselves with their duty weapon while at work and were afraid to report the incident for fear of getting written up through their department. The first incident happened to one of my co-workers who at the time was a patrol sergeant who was attempting to checkout a taser gun way back in the day when you were issued one to carry from the radio room. The desk officer would turn on the device to check and make sure its internal battery was charged properly before handing it over to the employee. The only problem was the desk officer had his finger on the trigger when he turned on the device, the taser gun discharged accidentally, striking the supervisor in the leg with one or two of the darts which shoot out of the weapon. The supervisor took a fifty-thousand-volt ride for that little boo-boo and probably both police officers had brown spots in their underwear that day!

22. HELP, I'VE BEEN SHOT (PART 2)

The second incident happened at a local pistol range, where a D.A. investigator accidentally shot himself in the hand while cleaning his gun after their annual gun qualification. He didn't want the authorities at the range to find out where he had actually shot himself because he was afraid the pistol range might not let them (his agency) continue to use their facility in the future. So, I am minding my own business driving up the freeway towards town on a busy Friday afternoon with bumper to bumper traffic. I am flagged down by two panicked men in a pick-up truck. I see the passenger is holding up his right hand, which is wrapped in a white t-shirt that is soaked in blood, and he screams to me that he is a police officer who has been accidentally shot. I ask him if he needs me to call him an ambulance. He immediately appears angered by my response. They attempt to drive away from me and get only about fifty feet ahead of me before getting stuck in the heavy traffic on the Freeway. I pull up to their truck again to ask them where they are attempting to go for medical treatment and he yells out to me, "Methodist Hospital." So, I use my emergency equipment to part the red sea (move traffic/open a lane) and advise my police dispatcher that I am escorting an injured officer (accidental gunshot wound) to the hospital. I also tell the dispatcher to notify the hospital of our E.T.A. and the condition of the officer involved. I get them to the hospital in record time and then he jumps out of the truck and runs into the emergency room without even one thanks. I never see and/or hear from the guy again. Wow, you would think he could have taken the time to say thanks or bought me lunch!

23. D.O.A.

One of the worst calls a police officer can get is one involving death. I remember being dispatched to a natural D.O.A. (natural causes) at a condo property. I was met by the landlady. She tells me that a foul odor is coming from the location and the person living there has not been seen or heard from in several weeks. The individual also has a history of poor health and was in and out of the hospital all the time. She unlocks the front door for me and says at the last minute, "There should be a large dog, a golden retriever, inside." I enter the location and I am immediately greeted by the large very friendly dog who is trying to run out the door. I grab the dog by his collar and ask the landlady to hold on to him while I go inside the location to check things out. I find the owner D.O.A. inside the house and see that his right arm is missing from the elbow down. There is no sign of forced entry, the home is not ransacked, and nothing appears to be missing. I have seen these types of calls before where the owner has died, and nobody is around to feed their pet. Naturally, the pet gets hungry. I am guessing the dog in this case after several weeks alone with the deceased owner, got hungry and did what he needed to do to survive. I make my necessary notifications to the Homicide division and the Medical Examiner's office advising them of the condition of the complainant as well as describing the crime scene. I go back outside, and the landlady tells me the deceased has no living relatives to contact and asks me what will happen to the dog? I tell her that Animal Control will be contacted and will likely take possession of the animal. She then asks since she is the landlady, if she could take the dog instead.

I hesitantly agree to her request so that I do not have to spend extra time waiting at the crime scene for Animal Control.

I go back to my patrol car and in the driveway to complete my supplement report as I wait for the body car and Homicide division (crime scene investigator) to arrive. The landlady is still hanging around my car holding on to the dog and I hear her say, "Here comes one of my nosey neighbors. I hate that woman." The lady walks up the driveway and leans down to pet the dog, allowing him to lick her all over her face, while asking us what is going on at the location. I thought to myself, "Lady you would not let that dog lick you in the face if you knew what he just ate!" Anyway, I am trying to tune out their conversation, as my window is down and trying to get my report done so I can get the heck out of there. The nosey neighbor asks the landlady about the owner of the dog and learns the owner is dead. The landlady then out of the blue asks the neighbor if she wants to keep the dog. I hear this conversation going south very quickly and I think to myself, "Oh boy. Why did I not just call Animal Control in the first place so I could avoid getting myself in this situation?" Then I see both ladies walk off with the "arm eating dog" in tow back to the nosey neighbor's house with her newfound furry four-legged friend. I cannot help but think, "What if that dog takes a big ole dump in this lady's backyard, and out pops an arm?"

24.   MAKE NEW FRIENDS AND CHOKE THEM

I had a call once to pick up a suspect from the Homicide division and transport him to the hospital for a mental health evaluation. The suspect was a white male, approximately forty years of age. He had for some reason felt like he might hurt himself or someone else. He even made statements threatening the President of The United States and had called the U.S. Secret Service prior to turning himself into HPD.

I pick up this guy from the Homicide division and transport him to Ben Taub Hospital. The guy was very cooperative and very polite the entire time. We arrive at the hospital and I am told by staff that we will be waiting a while before he can be admitted, so we go hang out together in one of the hallways. My pager goes off, so I tell the guy to not move while I walk approximately twenty to twenty-five feet away and make a phone call (I did not have a cell phone). As soon as I get on the phone, I hear a commotion down the hallway where I had left this guy. I look down there and he has both of his hands rapped around another man's throat like he is strangling him. I drop the phone and go running to him thinking he has just snapped and is trying to murder someone. I reach for my expandable baton and get ready to put some lumps on this guy's head. When I get there, he immediately tells me the other man was just walking by him and started having a seizure. Instead of just helping him to the floor, my guy grabs him around the throat and lets him hang there in mid-air with his feet almost off the ground. I tell him to let go of the man and the poor guy having the seizure drops to the ground like a sack of potatoes. Lucky for me, no one got hurt during the incident and both men got the necessary medical treatment they needed.

25. ALL POLICE CARS LOOK ALIKE

Police officers have bad days too!! Example, our police cars all look alike and when you all work in the same division as the K-9 detail with other police officers, all the vehicles are almost identical. The only difference is our agency would place a small shop number on the back window and/or bumper area to be able to identify each car. During my regular shift one day I parked my police car in the parking lot as usual and had my back turned in the opposite direction. I was minding my own business and cleaning some equipment outside on a picnic table. My police car was left unlocked because, in my mind, who would attempt to steal a K-9 car with a vicious canine inside it? Besides, I was only twenty to twenty-five feet away. Suddenly out of the blue, I hear someone screaming bloody murder for help in the parking lot. It sounded to me like a female being attacked due to the high-pitched sounding squeaky voice. I turned around very quickly to see two police dogs fighting each other and fur flying all over the parking lot. I also see a K-9 supervisor (male officer) attempting to pull his dog away from the fight and get to safety. I pause for a moment and try to figure out what is going on because none of this is making any sense. One of the canines in the fight looks like my dog, but I knew the last time I saw him, he was safe and sound inside the back of my car. I then quickly realize that it is my dog and he is kicking the other dog's butt very badly. The supervisor had been back spinning, attempting to get his dog out of the fight and was forced up against a horse barn with no place to go while screaming his lungs out! Other police officers including myself come running towards the danger to assist in breaking up the in-progress fight and help get the dogs separated.

After all the fur has cleared, I was still confused and trying to figure out how my dog got out of the police car in the first place? I was later told the supervisor had been out walking his dog in the parking lot and opened the back door to the wrong police car, thinking it was his car by mistake. I am sure that supervisor had a brown spot in his underwear that day!

26. CHEAP TRICKS

Police officers love playing tricks on each other and some have tried to be highly creative during their acts of mischief. In one incident, an officer tied the shoelaces together of another officer who was sleeping during roll call. While hanging out at the police station, you will learn very quickly to not leave your uniform shirt "unattended" or you might find that your badge has been turned upside down, or your name tag is missing. Sometimes officers would get outside help from a friendly wrecker driver and tow off an unsuspecting officer's police car during a lunch break to make him think it had been stolen. Some would take rubber bands and tie them around the police radio mic and crank up the good time radio on high volume so that when the car was started, the officer would be immediately "Live" on the two-way radio for all to hear him or her getting a little upset. They might also add some spice to the mischief by placing fingerprint powder inside the a/c vents and set the unit on high for them to get a face full of black powder. One officer I know even used a fire hose inside a parking garage to water down another unsuspecting officer's police car when they arrived at the location and accidentally flooded the garage in the process. I have also heard stories of officer's not liking another co-worker on their shift and doing something evil to his or her police car like placing a dead animal under the hood or seat of the vehicle to make the smell unbearable.

A SWAT officer got some serious payback by his co-workers one day out at the police academy after he had accidently run over and killed a duck in the parking lot. After the hit and run accident had been discovered, one of his co-workers captured a live duck and placed it inside his city ride with all the windows left cracked (quacked) open. The SWAT officer was not happy when he returned hours later to his vehicle and found a live duck along with copious amounts of bird poop all over the inside of his police car!

27. SHINY SHOES

Sometimes even our well-respected doctors in the community make mistakes and come to the attention of the police. For example, years ago I wrote a doctor a ticket for making an illegal turn (Main at Elgin). He fought the ticket in court. During his testimony at trial he tells the jury that he was on a medical emergency driving to Ben Taub Hospital. The only problem was he was driving in the wrong direction away from the hospital when I stopped him. The jury found him guilty and he had to pay a small fine. What's funny is after the trial was over an elderly woman who was on the jury came up to me and says, "I knew that doctor was lying and you were telling the truth after I looked down at your shoes and saw how shiny they were." Note to self, always wear "shiny shoes" to court.

28. MEDICAL EMERGENCY

I happen to stop another doctor years later for making an illegal turn off Kirby drive. He told me that he was on a medical emergency. This guy believed he was above the law and did not have time for a ticket. He had an awfully bad attitude and demanded that I give him a police escort (red lights and siren) to the Women's Hospital located in southwest Houston. At this point, I am thinking this is crazy, but I will play his little game and ask a supervisor for permission to provide him with an escort hoping they would "deny" my request. Just as my luck would have it, a supervisor approves my silly request over the two-way radio and off we go driving the speed limit. This guy stays behind me driving his car while I am clearing all the motor traffic and red lights using my emergency equipment until reaching our destination. We park in the parking lot and the doctor attempts to bolt past me into the hospital, but I cut him off just before he reaches the building with my ticket book in hand and request his autograph for the original violation. I give him his copy of the ticket and he thinks that we are done. I then tell him how bad I feel about having to write him a ticket and I want to help him out. At this point, he has a very confused look on his face as he is walking quickly towards the hospital front doors to get away from me and I am like in his back pocket. I tell him that I am going to verify that he was on a medical emergency inside the hospital and then maybe get the ticket dismissed. He is now running into the hospital towards the elevator and he yells at me saying, "You can't go with me. I'm headed to surgery." I tell him no problem, as I am going straight to the administration office to speak to someone who can verify his employment at the location. I go into the main office and I tell this nice lady working there that I am trying to help this poor doctor out who got a ticket. She asks me for the doctor's name and attempts to look him up on their computer system. I then find out he did not even work at the hospital, but his wife did. Boom!! I call the D.A.'s office for charges against the doctor for making a false police report and charges are accepted. I walk the charges thru at the D.A.'s office myself and wait several days for a judge to sign the warrant. After not hearing anything for almost a week I start calling the D.A.'s intake office almost every day, talking to different assistant D.A.'s and none can give me a straight answer as to why a judge won't sign the warrant. Finally, I get one of them to tell me (confidentially) that because the violator in the case was a doctor that none of the judges would sign the warrant.

29.   CANINE CONTACT

One thing K-9 handlers do not like talking about is the dreaded accidental canine contact (dog bite) and it happens no matter how careful you are with your canine. Our dogs have accidentally bit mailmen delivering the mail, children playing ball outside at school, citizens during routine traffic stops, a person of interest inside a Motel room, lots of homeless people, family members, and numerous police officers who were just at the right place at the wrong time. During the seventeen years I spent in the K-9 detail I had approximately three dogs. My first police dog bit me accidentally eight times over an eight-year period that we worked as a team together and I never blamed the dog for any of them. In fact, I considered all of them "handler error" due to whatever I was doing at the time that made the dog bite me in the first place. My second police dog bit me only twice and my third police dog bit me only one time! As you can tell, I became a better dog handler as the years went by and the injuries became fewer.

What I will never forget is the five Houston police officers that my canines accidentally bit during my tour of duty in the K-9 detail and the pain it caused all of us. Believe it or not, two of the patrol officers who were injured had the same last name. I was beginning to think my dog was reading their name tags. In fact, I got so paranoid that I started reading officer's name tags on scenes and made sure their last name was not the same as the two previously injured police officers.

30. UNHAPPY CUSTOMER

One day while searching an old, abandoned crack house, I found a small wallet size picture of an attractive female and for whatever reason kept it as a joke. During a call for service not long after that I had to make an arrest and take a male suspect to the city jail. During the transport to the city jail the suspect became angry at me for the arrest and told me that he was considering making a complaint. I opened my wallet and showed him the picture I had found inside the old, abandoned building. I told him it was a picture of my wife and how disappointed everyone involved would be if that happened. Believe it or not, his attitude changed almost immediately, and he apologized for his actions. I thought to myself how amazing that a simple little picture could change someone's attitude so quickly and end his anger. The issue was instantly resolved.

31.   DOING THE CHICKEN

One of my co-workers told me about the first shooting that he was involved in as a police officer and after hearing the story I was not sure I would have shared the information with anyone. He tells me that a felony warrant was being run at a house and as soon as the front door was kicked-in, a shootout occurred between the officers and the suspect. He says the suspect is hiding behind a bed in his bedroom shooting at them and the officers are standing in the doorway returning fire. My co-worker is standing next to another officer that is shooting a Colt .45 semi-auto pistol and all the shell casings are ejecting towards him. One of the hot shell casings goes down the backside of his shirt and he thinks that he has been shot. He immediately drops to the floor and starts rolling around doing the chicken and yelling that he has been shot. At least forty rounds have been fired between the officers and the suspect, but remarkably no one has been hit. After all the smoke clears and the suspect is in custody, the officers start checking on my co-worker to find out the extent of his injuries. He tells me they ripped off his shirt and bullet-proof vest looking for his gunshot wound only to find an empty shell casing! He is totally embarrassed by the entire incident and his fellow officers give him all kinds of grief over his strange reaction.

32. TWO CANDY BARS

When I was a rookie, one of the police officers who I rode with was a shorter looking man who had obvious weight issues and a big tummy. To me, he looked like a giant balloon with a rubber band tied around the middle due to the way his gun belt fit around his body and he looked funny wearing his uniform. Instead of carrying extra bullets in his spare ammo cases, he would carry two snickers candy bars. I once asked him why he did that and he told me, "You never know when you might get tied down at a SWAT situation."

33. FART COMPLAINT

Getting called into the sergeant's office due to a citizen complaint is never any fun. One of my old partners had to go see the desk sergeant once because he intentionally farted on a combative acting complainant. The sergeant asked him for his side of the story and then told him the next time that he needed to "relieve" himself to not make it so obvious by making unnecessary noises, like grunting, while lifting his leg and turning his butt cheeks toward the complainant at the same time.

34. CREATIVE TICKET WRITING

Sometimes citizens are not incredibly happy about getting traffic tickets and some can have an attitude with the officer involved. One of my co-workers who was very creative would draw a circle around the "x" next to the line where the violator had to sign the ticket making it look like a tiny ass if they had given him a hard time. He would also write in big bold letters "LLPOF" (liar, liar, pants on fire) on the bottom of the ticket if he felt they were lying to him about their unbelievable excuse. He told me that he had to go to court to testify regarding one of those tickets after it was contested by a violator and the defense attorney questioned the officer on the witness stand about the suspicious bold letters printed on the ticket. According to him, everyone in the court room cracked up laughing after he had to testify and explained what the letters meant. Also, way back in the day (before my time), I was told some police officers would even place boogers on the ticket or sneeze on it like it was a Kleenex and then hand it to the uncooperative violator just to add insult to injury. DNA and the Coronavirus would not permit that today!

35. DAYTONA 500

One day while I am driving home on the freeway in my marked K-9 car, I spot two vehicles racing each other going in and out of traffic. When they see me both vehicles slow down enough to not bring attention to them-selves and are acting all cool since they see the police. I can tell they are both in a hurry and just waiting for me to take an exit or go a different route so that both can continue their little Daytona 500 car race on the freeway. I pull up next to both vehicles with my emergency lights activated and get on the P.A. system and tell both drivers to knock off the car race or someone is going to get a ticket. We then drive a short distance up the freeway and one of the cars takes an exit towards the IAH Airport while the other violator involved continues driving in the same direction as my vehicle, but at the posted speed limit. I cannot prove it, but I am sure these young fellas knew each other and were probably talking to one another on their cell phones during the entire incident.

I am thinking the racing incident is all over and continue driving home minding my own business. I glance out the passenger side window and see one of the cars (black Chevrolet Camaro) that was racing on the free-way. He is driving on the feeder road parallel to my vehicle on the freeway and his driver side window is down. The guy has got his arm fully extended out the window and he is flipping me off big time. He then punches the accelerator and I see him take off like a rocket driving maybe one hundred mph and the speed limit is forty-five mph. Well crap, what do I do now? I can (A) ignore this guy and keep driving home or (B) chase after him. I would have to drive off the freeway, through the grass to gain access to the feeder road (there was no exit) where I last saw him speed off and attempt to find him. I decided to go ahead and attempt to locate the violator. In my mind, if he gets away with it now, he will repeat it again later! I also felt like someone should teach this guy a lesson and not be so disrespectful to law enforcement personnel. With that being said, I am wondering if this guy is long gone or was it vaguely possible that he got stuck somewhere in heavy traffic along JFK Boulevard? I start driving toward the airport and what do I see sitting at a red light, but a black Chevrolet Camaro with my suspect behind the wheel. I bet he got a little brown spot in his underwear after seeing a police car in his rearview mirror. I light the guy up when the light turned green and he pulls over immediately. I walk up to his vehicle and politely ask for his driver's license and proof of insurance. I then ask him about the rude middle finger gesture (giving me the bird) and he tells me, oh it was not meant for you officer, it was meant for the other car that he was racing! Well, I was born at night, but it was not last night. I wrote this guy about three different tickets and I thought he was going to cry. I also wrote on the bottom of the ticket in big bold letters "LLPOF" (liar, liar, pants on fire).

36. WHEN I WAS A GEMINI

I once stopped a person of interest who was possibly involved in a crime in my patrol area and asked him during the interview if he was ever arrested before. He responds, "Only when I was a Gemini." He says "Gemini" instead of saying a juvenile. Well, alrighty then!

37. POLICE GRAFFITI

Back in the day, our police cars use to be all white and I inherited a hand-me-down K-9 car (senior officers got the newer cars) from an old veteran officer who was retiring. He carried around a can of white spray paint and anytime he would hit something with one of the bumpers, he would just spray paint over the damage. The only reason I know this is because he left me one of the empty spray cans in the car and you could see all the running paint marks on both bumpers (front & rear) which had dried over the old damage.

38. TIMMY-NO

When I worked in the K-9 detail, we had a canine named "Timmy" (not his real name). His named rhymed with that name and he would not listen to his handler so you would always hear the handler saying, "Timmy-no." We made a joke about it and said that he now officially had two first names instead of one. That dog was crazy and would do whatever he wanted regardless if the K-9 handler approved or not. We trained our canines every Tuesday and everybody was always waiting to see how Timmy-no would mess up. One time another canine was doing bite work on the sleeve and Timmy-no observed what was happening, he somehow escaped from his handler and joined in on the action (two dogs on one bite sleeve is a no-no). If Timmy-no saw another canine out taking a pee break or playing ball, he would somehow find a way to break away from his handler and try to join them. That dog also loved to hump people and his handler thought it was funny to watch, so the bad behavior was never corrected until it got out of control.

The handler went out-of-town once, and officers on each shift had to take care of Timmy-no at our police kennels. I turned my back on Timmy-no for just a brief second while using my cell phone and I got blind-sighted (struck from behind) by what felt like a freight train. Before

I knew what hit me, Timmy-no was humping my leg from behind (where I could not get to him) while gripping me tightly with his front legs and would not let go. After a short period of time fighting with him without a leash, I finally got him to disengage and felt like I needed to get a case number for sexual assault. Dang crazy Malinois!

39. I'M A JUVENILE

When I transferred to the K-9 detail, I worked on the night shift for four years and got involved in some crazy stuff. One night, I checked by on a burglary-in-progress call at a bar on Washington Avenue. When the primary unit arrived on scene, the suspects took off in a stolen van. A short police chase ends quickly when the suspect's vehicle wrecks and hits a telephone pole. Two suspects then jumped out of the vehicle and start running on foot. I see the driver take off running like a deer, towards a large field from a side road. I deploy my canine partner after the suspect refuses to stop. This bad guy is probably at least a hundred yards away from us and I am shining my flashlight in his direction to show my police canine where he went. The canine finally sees the suspect while he is running in the distance away from us and the dog takes off like a missile locked in on its target. The canine reaches the fleeing suspect and knocks him off his feet. The dog has him by the booty and the suspect starts yelling at me from a distance, "I'm a juvenile, I'm a juvenile." I finally get there to pull the dog off him and take him into custody. I get the guy back to the patrol car and find out that he is not a juvenile. Instead he turned out to be a grown man that is twenty years old.

40. ASSIST THE SECURITY GUARDS

I was once dispatched to a call involving two security guards who were patrolling an apartment complex in their patrol vehicle and got attacked by a crazy naked guy on drugs. They told me that he jumped on top of their car and started crashing out the front windshield with his bare feet. They get out of the car and the fight was on. When I arrive, both security guards are on top of this butt naked guy and they are trying their best to hold him down on the ground. The security guards' uniforms are ripped to shreds. They are beat to a pulp and covered in blood. As I walk up to them, one of the guards looks at me and asks if they should let go of him and let him up? I responded by saying, "Nope, just hold on to what you got" and I handed him a pair of handcuffs. I requested an ambulance to the scene to check out both the security guards and the suspect. The crazy guy later dies at the hospital from the unknown drugs he ingested in addition to the lengthy fight with the guards and possibly having a heart attack or stroke. Later, I go and give a statement in the Homicide division regarding the incident.

The security guards are eventually cleared in the case and are not charged. A female homicide detective who took my statement during the investigation, later asks me if I really did say what I said in my above statement to the security guards? I responded, "Yep!"

41. FREE POPSICLES

While working in patrol, I was once dispatched to an accident on the Southwest Freeway involving an overturned ice cream truck with a lot of the contents spilled out on the roadway. When I finally get there, I see at least five wrecker drivers parked on the side of the freeway and all of them standing outside of their trucks in a straight line (almost at attention). They are holding popsicles in both hands! One of them asks me if they can eat them because they are going to melt anyways and then had the nerve to ask me if I wanted to eat one. I just shook my head and ignored them.

42. BIG OLE MISUNDERSTANDING

Working for the police department as a police officer, they allow you to work side jobs that are completed either on your days off or any time that you are basically not on duty (burning time) and/or available other than during your regular assigned shift. Officers get accustomed to working these side jobs to supplement their income, and sometimes rely on them way too much to pay for their expensive new toys (fancy cars and fishing boats). Police officers also sometimes forget that their loyalty to the department always comes first and that their employer is the one that affords them the privilege to be able to work these side jobs.

For example, back in the 1990s, another officer and I are working together on patrol running radar and attempt to stop a car for speeding, but he does not stop for us and the chase is on! We advise the police dispatcher via police two-way radio of the incident and continue to give updates as to our current location throughout the chase. This bad guy is driving crazy (they usually do), going through people's yards, tearing up their grass, and damaging miscellaneous property along the way. Not to mention, the suspect is putting the general public and pursuing police officers in danger of serious bodily injury or death during this event while he does everything possible to evade arrest. The chase goes on for several more miles and ends up stopping behind the building of a grocery store. We jump out of the police car and draw down on the suspect who is still sitting in the car with his hands out the driver side window. All of a sudden, we see our off-duty patrol sergeant who was working an extra job for the business, appear from the back door of the grocery story loading ramp. He is waving his arms while running toward us yelling, "Put down your guns." We are very confused about his unusual actions and are attempting to figure out what the heck is going on? He tells us that our suspect is the son of his employer at the grocery store and that all of this is a big misunderstanding! We handcuff the suspect and place him in the rear of the police car and are still attempting to sort things out. I am still a little upset over the entire incident, and my partner goes to speak with our off-duty supervisor. We later find out this location (grocery store) was our sergeant's regular extra job and his employer was also a respected Houston lawyer who owned the business. The suspect (the lawyer's son) is not so well known and was basically a loser! Our supervisor again tells us that this entire incident is just a big misunderstanding and that he will sort out the whole thing himself. My partner and I are both stunned about what just happened and are both scratching our heads over the deal. They don't train you in the police academy for this kind of stuff and I'm pretty sure the supervisor in this case was stepping over the line a little bit, showing more loyalty towards his extra job than for his responsibility and loyalty to the police department. We end up leaving the suspect with our off-duty supervisor to manage the scene from his extra job and we return to service never to hear anything about the incident again. Wow, that was too crazy of an incident for me to comprehend that big ole misunderstanding!

43. SOY SAUCE

One day while working in the K-9 detail I was dispatched to an alarm call with forced entry on a large warehouse containing restaurant supplies. Myself along with another K-9 officer arrive on the scene and I deploy my canine to search the building. About halfway thru the search we spot a large puddle of soy sauce that had been spilled all over the concrete floor and just about the same time my canine comes flying around a corner towards the mess. I panic and yell at the dog commanding him to stop, but it was too late. The canine puts on the brakes and slides into the soy sauce. I felt like I was watching a train wreck in slow motion as he rolled completely over into this big mess and gets it all over him from head to toe. He jumps back up and attempts to shake it all off, but it is soaked into his fur like a sponge. He is covered in this nasty smelling sauce and there is not a water hose in sight. I later grabbed a spare towel that I had in the police car and attempted to wipe some of it off before letting him into the car. Have you ever seen a ninety-pound long-haired German Shepherd police dog covered in soy sauce? On a positive note his coat sure was soft and shiny after I gave him a bath!

44.   WHERE IS YOUR HAT?

"Where is your hat?" "Go get your hat!" When I was a young rookie, we would hear this over and over from our supervisors almost daily and it got old very quickly. Someone in the higher ranks decided one day that supervisors should start enforcing our General Orders/Rules Manual regarding wearing our department issued police hats whenever we were on duty, in uniform and outside of the patrol vehicle. This meant wearing your police hat everywhere you went out in public, such as on a call for service, writing a ticket, directing traffic, on your lunch break, and/or attending a funeral. It was hard to remember to put the dang thing on every time you got out of the car. You were rolling the dice if you decided to not wear it. If you got caught without it by a supervisor, they would threaten to write you up! One of my co-workers told me that one time he was dispatched to a busy intersection to direct traffic due to the traffic lights malfunctioning and he did not have his hat with him. After about fifteen minutes, his supervisor shows up on the scene and walks out into the middle of the busy street and immediately tells my co-worker to go get his hat. Most officers would leave their hats in the trunk of the car and/or back at the police station inside their locker. The hats looked terrible and were in poor condition due to getting all squashed by other equipment you were required to carry, and they were dirty looking from being in the trunk all day (we looked like bus drivers wearing them). My co-worker had accidentally left his hat at home that day and he lived approximately thirty miles away from the police station. He did not bother to tell his supervisor that it would take him over an hour to retrieve his hat from the house and return to his traffic assignment. The supervisor was left directing traffic in the hot Houston heat for a lot longer than he thought while my co-worker followed the verbal orders he was given by his boss.

45. THE MISSING FINGER

Police K-9 teams face a lot of battles together and hopefully win more than they lose. We were requested to check by with southwest patrol units who were looking for a burglary suspect in the neighborhood. They were having trouble locating him. We start searching for this guy going yard to yard on a hot summer's day. After almost an hour, we are really getting tired. There are only two houses left to check in the block. We press on, not wanting this guy to get away. As we walk into the backyard, the police dog throws his head up and starts pulling me towards a large shed. The canine crawls through a bunch of overgrown weeds, vines, and sticker bushes while pulling me to the back side of the shed. When we get in there, I can see the suspect who is crouched down and holding a large piece of sheet metal. The suspect jumps up and attempts to hit both of us with the large object in his hands by swinging it back and forth like a sword. The canine grabs one of the suspect's legs which causes him to drop his weapon. Now the suspect attempts to strangle the canine with both hands around his neck and I am throwing punches to get him to release the dog. Somehow, the suspect breaks free and attempts to run from us towards the back side of the house. By now, at least four or five officers are in the backyard and put the guy on the ground.

While handcuffing the suspect, one of the rookie officers' yells over to me and says, "He is missing a finger." I walk over there and sure enough, I see his middle finger has been bitten off. They call for an ambulance to check the suspect out and provide first-aid. The suspect is transported to the hospital and charges are filed against him. One of the young rookie officers on the scene later told me that when the canine was chasing the suspect through the backyard, the dog ran between the police officers' legs and never attempted to bite him. His eyes were so big when he told me that story and he was completely amazed the police dog did not bite him! We attempted to locate the suspect's missing finger at the scene but were not successful finding it. I wondered if whenever my dog took his next big poop if the missing finger would show back up.

46. INJURED ON DUTY

Sometime during your career as a police officer, you will get injured on duty either by chasing a suspect and/or fighting with one who does not want to go to jail. I have had a few small cuts, sprains, dog bites, and bruises over the years. Most of the time, no one from the department will ever attempt to contact you (unless you have been shot or seriously injured) regarding a minor boo-boo and they allow you to deal with it yourself. I once had a call regarding a burglary suspect who ran from some officers and hid underneath a house. My police canine finds the guy and crawls under the house to get him. The suspect grabs a brick and throws it at my dog, striking him in the head. The police dog is stunned for a moment, and then makes canine contact with the suspect. We get the guy into custody and I take my canine to the city veterinarian for his minor injury. The police dog is checked out and released with only small cut, bumps, and bruises. The funny part is, as I said before, whenever I got hurt in the past nobody ever called to check-up on me and I am okay with that. However, when my canine got hurt on the job, I must have received fifteen to twenty phone calls from officers all over the department including the Chief's office, wanting to know if my canine was okay and what the extent of his injuries were from the incident.

47. K-9 DEMO

Lots of folks do not know what K-9 teams are used for, and we get requests for demonstrations (K-9 demo) at churches, schools, and community events throughout the city. Most of the time, they go off without a hitch, but sometimes strange things happen that are not planned. One such time happened after an event was over and a gentleman approached the K-9 handler to ask a few questions. He then asked if he could pet the dog and the handler reluctantly agreed. The guy starts petting the dog and then bends down unexpectedly to give the police dog a kiss on the muzzle (bad idea). The dog goes into defense mode and bites the guy on his nose and lips. The guy seeks medical treatment for his injury and then later attempts to call the police station to make a complaint. The only problem is the guy's lips are swollen (maybe a few stitches) and when he talks, he sounds like a drunk who has been out drinking all night. The guy then starts calling the police station and the desk sergeant continues hanging up on him, thinking he is drunk because he cannot understand what he is saying. If you are going to be dumb, you better be tough!

48. POLICE WAR STORIES

Police officers love telling war stories. One of my co-workers who ate lunch with me at Luby's Cafeteria was one of the best. Some people would call him crazy, and others would say he was just a little bit strange. I am not sure what he was, but he sure could tell a great story and lived an interesting life.

Everybody called him "Bart" because he looked a lot like a cartoon character on a popular television show. He was an intelligent guy who patrolled an area of Houston that had a Buddhist temple. The monks basically took him in. They taught him how to speak their language fluently and he was used by the police department to translate for officers whenever he was needed. He also told me that he lived all alone in an old airplane hangar on the south side of Houston and taught himself how to fly in his two home-made airplanes made from build-it-yourself kits! Could you imagine taking off on your first solo flight not knowing if you would make it off the ground and/or be able to land it safely? He said one time he was flying towards Conroe, Texas and ran out of gas mid-air. He did not have a two-way radio and he had to make an emergency landing inside a U.S. Army Reserve Center. He said when he landed the plane, all the soldiers came running outside towards him fearing they were under attack. He said in the end they were all very polite to him and even gave him gas for his plane.

He also liked to jump out of airplanes (hopefully wearing a parachute), but soon got bored with that so he started base-jumping off mountain cliffs and very tall buildings. He told me that one time he was overseas and they were going to pay him fifteen thousand dollars to jump off the top of a building for a T.V. commercial with some other base-jumpers, but he didn't have an extra job permit (officers are required to get a permit to work an outside job) and couldn't reach the HPD Extra Employment division by phone, so he did the jump for free! During another adventure, he climbed up a very tall mountain with one of his base-jumper friends. It took them almost all day to get to the top. When they reached the top of the mountain, the weather got bad and the fog was so thick, they were afraid to jump. After debating about the bad situation, both decide to go ahead and jump. His friend goes first and just by the unusual sounds he heard (parachute did not deploy), he could tell his friend did not make it to the very bottom alive. My co-worker tells me that he did not feel like walking all the way back down the mountain by himself since it took them so long to get up there and it was getting dark. He decides to go ahead and jump anyways, even though his friend had just died. According to him base-jumping, is a dangerous hobby and your friendships are short lived due to them dying off very quickly.

49.   RECKLESS DRIVING

We were given a direct order once to monitor traffic at major intersections and write traffic tickets if any violations were observed. I am out there doing my job as ordered and observe a vehicle run a red light. I take off after the guy and use my emergency equipment (red/blue lights and siren) to pull him over, but he does not stop. The chase is on and this guy has got a long head start ahead of me and I am doing everything I can to catch up. There was also a lot of radio traffic at the time (other units talking to dispatch) and I was having a hard time even getting on the radio to advise the police dispatcher of my status in the chase. I am finally able to break the air on the police radio and put out the chase and additional units start heading my way. I keep following guy as he busts through red lights and stop signs along the route. The guy's car finally comes to a quick halt and he hurriedly jumps out and starts running toward a yellow cab that has stopped at an intersection/red light. I am not sure what this guy is doing and wondering if he is attempting to carjack the yellow cab driver. Several other units arrive on the scene and we all have our guns drawn. We approach the suspect who is now crawling into the back of the yellow cab. Again, my mind is going a hundred miles an hour and I am thinking the very worst scenario from my police training, is this now a hostage situation? The guy grabs a jacket from the back of the yellow cab and then comes out of the vehicle with both his hands up in the air. Officers approach the unarmed man, conduct a quick pat-down search, and handcuff him. After the situation is under control, we finally learn why the guy was chasing the yellow cab, which just moments before had dropped him and some friends off at his house. He tells us that he accidentally left his jacket in the rear of the yellow cab. The cabbie took off not knowing the property was left inside the vehicle. The guy also swore that he had tunnel vision while chasing down the yellow cab and was unaware the police were behind him a half block back, attempting to stop him. Oh boy, what a mess! After the dust cleared, I felt sorry for the guy after learning what had happened and did not want to take him to jail for reckless driving. One of my supervisors who was on duty at the time checked-by the scene and basically ordered me to call the District Attorney's office for possible criminal charges instead of writing the poor guy a few tickets. That bad little decision he made to chase down the yellow cab turned out to be an expensive lesson for him, and not exceptionally good news for his driving record.

50.   ROOFTOP PURSUIT

We had a car chase in northwest Houston once, and after the suspect crashed his vehicle, he ran off into the neighborhood. The officer's set-up a perimeter and called for a K-9 unit. I arrive quickly and start going yard to yard looking for this guy. My dog locates the suspect who is hiding on the roof of a house and he refuses to come down. One of my co-workers, who weighs about one hundred fifty pounds grabs a ladder and climbs up there to confront the suspect who is twice his size. The suspect sees the officer approaching him and starts running away. We now have a rooftop foot pursuit with the suspect jumping from one rooftop to another rooftop and my co-worker is following right behind him. This whole thing looks like a scene from a mission impossible movie because I have never seen a police officer in real life chasing a suspect on foot and they are jumping from rooftop to rooftop! My friend gets close enough to tackle the suspect and they both go tumbling down from the top of the roof to the ground below. The suspect is taken into custody unharmed and the police officer limps away with a sprained ankle.

51. MY FIRST MENTAL CASE

Back in the early 1980s, I had my first encounter with a mental case, and it turned out to be a very scary situation. I had a partner that day and we volunteered to check-by on a disturbance call around the 1500 block of Caroline Street. The call slip stated that an individual who had just been released from Ben Taub Hospital Psychiatric Ward had broken fifteen hundred dollars' worth of glass at a local business and was still on the scene. We get there quickly and see the suspect who is standing in the middle of the street with his arms stretched straight up above his head and he is holding two sixteen-ounce ball peen hammers in his hands. It is about 9:00 p.m. at night and we drive up close enough to use our spotlight to light him up. This guy has got a glazed look on his face and he is completely frozen where he is standing. We use the police car PA system and order the suspect to drop his weapons and get on the ground. The suspect refuses to obey our commands and starts walking slowly towards the front of our police car. We exit the patrol car and draw down on the suspect. Surely, he will comply once he sees we mean business. We are now yelling at the suspect at the top of our lungs and we still have our guns drawn at him. He continues to get closer and closer to our car until he reaches the front bumper and stops. Suddenly, the guy screams out loud like Tarzan and begins crashing out our front headlights with the two hammers. We did not have Tasers back then or any other type of less lethal weapon at our disposal and this guy had us both feeling like we had a brown spot in our underwear. I looked at my partner and tell him to get back into the patrol car and we start backing up very slowly while watching the suspect follow us. We get on the two-way police radio and request back-up right away! Another unit arrives from the opposite direction, and now the suspect is focused totally on him while walking towards the front of his patrol car. I advise the other unit on the radio to back out away from the suspect due to him still being armed and the damage he had already done to our police car. So, all I can see is this panicked look on this police officer who is desperately attempting to put his car in reverse (shifter was on the column on the old Fords) to escape and he can't find it fast enough! The suspect walks right up to the front bumper of the second police car and crashes out his headlights. Now we have two damaged police cars with no headlights, and the suspect is still on the loose in the middle of the street. Additional units quickly arrive on the scene and assist in corralling the suspect between the police car bumpers to prevent him from escaping. The suspect realized that he had no place to go and dropped his weapons. My sergeant arrives on the scene and sees the suspect is in custody and no longer a threat. I immediately tell my supervisor what action was taken to prevent having to kill this guy and he tells me that I should have somehow ended the situation quicker.

52.   FTO AND THE TRAINEE

Back in the old days when I was a FTO at the Central Patrol Station, I was assigned a rookie. His last name was not hard to remember because I am originally from the same great southern State. He was a very funny guy and I liked him from the start because of his personality. One day, during FTO training, I let him drive the police car for the very first time since he graduated from the police academy and he is all excited. Suddenly without warning, as we are driving down a main roadway, he turns the steering wheel sharply to the left and attempts to make a quick U-turn in the middle of the street to avoid heavy traffic ahead of us. He runs over a small concrete divider which badly scraped the undercarriage of the police car and it sounded so bad I thought it took off the muffler. I look at him and asked why he did that. He responds back by saying, "Because we be the police."

53. CARS WITHOUT CAGES

When I first transferred to the K-9 detail, we did not have any cages in our cars for the dogs and some of the standard equipment inside the vehicle became a chew toy for the animals. One night as I walked past a K-9 vehicle in the parking lot I noticed the driver side seat in a co-worker's car was missing (no cloth or padding) and the only thing left were the wire springs. It looked like someone had literally set his car seat on fire! I walked into the police station and ask the K-9 officer what happened to his car seat and he tells me his dog ate it. I asked him why he did not get it fixed at the police garage, and he told me the dog would just do it again. This very same K-9 officer was missing half of one ear due to a police canine that bit it off after he sat down inside another K-9 handlers' car that did not have a cage. He was an ex-Marine who was tough as nails and one of the nicest guys you could ever meet. Most people would have taken off a long period of time from work (injured on duty) and had some type of reconstructive surgery done to their ear from the damage done by the police canine. Instead, he put a Band-aid on it and came back to work the next day or two. Oh, the officer's ear was never found, and they believe the police canine ate it!

54. WHITE "CRÈME" EVIDENCE

I once made the mistake of leaving a box of donuts on the front floorboard of the police K-9 car while I ran into the police station and used the restroom. When I return to the police car, I see the box had been ripped open and almost all the donuts were missing! I turn around to look at my canine partner who was hiding in the back seat and he had white crème filling (evidence) from the chocolate donuts all over his nose and muzzle. Guilty!!

55. FRESH PURSUIT

Anybody that has been in law enforcement any length of time has been involved in a lot of high-speed car chases and some of them you will never forget due to the level of craziness from the actions of the offender. One that I will never forget involved our narcotics detail that was doing an undercover investigation on a drug dealer who had just picked up thirteen kilos (bricks) of cocaine with street value of twenty-five thousand dollars for each brick. Things went from bad to worse very quickly after the drugs were picked up by the suspect in the area of southwest Houston and the undercover Narcotics officer's requested a marked patrol unit to make a traffic stop on his vehicle. The suspect, knowing that jail time was soon to be a reality for him, refused to stop and the chase was on!

This guy's game plan was to get rid of the evidence and escape capture at all cost. So, he starts driving like a crazy person attempting to run police cars off the road and throwing kilos (bricks) of cocaine out the window while driving over one hundred mph on the 288 South Freeway. If that were not bad enough, he also had a gallon jug of bug killer inside his car and thought he could destroy most of the evidence by pouring the bug killer over each individual kilo while he evaded arrest. The only problem was he was doing this while holding the "brick" in his lap prior to pitching them out the driver side window of his car which caused him to start overdosing. When the chase finally ended the suspect had passed out from being overdosed on the drugs and was foaming at the mouth. He was also having convulsions from the cocaine he ingested, and he had to be taken to a hospital via ambulance in Angleton, Texas for emergency medical treatment. They cut off his nasty, sticky clothes which had large clumps of cocaine mixed with dried bug killer all over his body prior to treating him and had to use copious amounts of Narcan to revive him from his self-induced drug overdose. The primary and secondary units in the chase had large amounts of cocaine stuck in the grill, headlights, and hood of their police cars. The Narcotic's division had to send out a Narcotic's officer to the scene to scrape off and recover all the drug evidence from the two police cars that were directly behind the suspect's vehicle during the chase. The suspect was later found guilty at his trial and was sent to prison for twenty-five years.

56. THE WRONG GUY

Sometimes the guilty flee even when the police are not even looking for them and run away just because they saw a police car in the area. We had a stolen motor vehicle chase in northeast Houston that ended near Deer Park, Texas and the driver fled the location on foot into a neighborhood. The patrol officer's set-up a perimeter very quickly to contain the suspect and requested a K-9 unit to the scene. Upon arrival, we obtain a brief description of the guy and start going yard to yard looking for the wanted suspect. After searching for almost an hour, a patrol officer tells me he saw someone running behind a house that had not been searched. I was thinking to myself, "Why didn't this officer give me this information at the beginning?" So, we head into the backyard area and the canine leads us toward a large shed. The canine circles the structure and begins to get excited, wanting to enter the location. I provide a K-9 verbal warning for anyone inside the location to surrender and get no response in return. The canine then goes into the location to search it and finds a suspect who was hiding underneath a wooden pallet covered with a blue tarp. It is wintertime and this guy is wearing a big thick coat and two pairs of pants like a bite suit. When the dog makes contact with this guy, he does not make a sound and does not appear to feel any type of pain or discomfort from the dog. I yell out verbal commands for the suspect to surrender and pull

the canine away from him, but he refuses to come out. The patrol officers finally rush in and take the uninjured suspect into custody. As we are
walking back to the police car, the primary unit in the chase walks up to
me and tells me what a great job my police dog did locating the bad guy
in the shed. Then he says, "Except for one small problem." I am looking
at him with a confused look on my face. He tells me the suspect who was
found hiding in the shed was not the same person that he observed driving
the stolen motor vehicle during the chase. I am really confused now about
the situation and my butt is starting to pucker a little bit because I do not
know why the guy ran away. The suspect was also mouthing off saying
we had arrested the wrong person and he was only trying to stay warm
while innocently sleeping inside the shed when we arrested him. I am like
freaking out a little thinking what the heck, did we just arrest an innocent
homeless person? Come to find out this suspect had a felony warrant out
for his arrest and when he observed all of the police cars arriving in the
area from the stolen car chase, he thought the police had come to get him!
His guilty conscious had gotten the best of him, so he decided to run away
and hide inside the shed.

57. THE ONE THAT GOT AWAY

Have you ever had one of those moments when something happens and you kind of tilt your head from side to side like dogs do when you're talking to them and they have this confused look on their face? I had lots of these moments over the years and would say to myself, "Did that really just happen?" Once, I was driving home late one night and saw a guy exceeding the speed limit (85/65 mph) and I drive up behind him. I activate my emergency lights in hopes he will get the message and slow down. As soon as I do this out of the corner of my left eye, I see another vehicle in the far-left lane (a red corvette) going probably one hundred eighty mph. He passes both of us at the speed of light. By the time I reach for my microphone to report the reckless driver in the corvette he is long gone and nowhere to be found. I have this mega second moment thinking to myself should I report this incident to dispatch or not and then go, oh heck no! He is long gone, and nobody could have caught him anyways! I quickly put down the microphone and continue driving home like nothing ever happened.

58. WRONG WAY DRIVER

Another time I was driving home and see a drunk driver coming head on in front of me as he drove the wrong way on the Hardy toll road. I activate my emergency lights and the guy slows down just enough to drive right next to my car and we are now facing each other (driver side window to driver side window). I yell out to the guy who is three sheets to the wind, "Hey dude, what are you doing?" You are going to get somebody killed and you are going the wrong way! He looks at me with this glazed look in his eyes and then drives off still going in the wrong direction. I quickly advise the police dispatch of the vehicle's description, last known location, and direction of travel. I even turned completely around on the toll road going with the flow of traffic attempting to re-locate the wrong way driver, but he was long gone.

59. FREEWAY MISHAPS

I will never forget leaving from work one night from the downtown Central Police Station and got on the freeway to drive home. It was pitch dark and as I rounded a curve my headlights light up an object in the middle of the freeway. I see this old drunk guy who is standing in the middle of the roadway with other cars zooming by all around him and he is just standing there with both of his fists up like he wants to fight all of the cars. The man must have had a guardian angel to get him off the freeway and not be killed that night. I've also seen people who have lost ladders, washing machines, couches, file cabinets, and a very large metal desk right in the middle of the freeway where they were left abandoned to be run over by unsuspecting drivers. I've seen cars lined up on the side of the freeway and all of them have got flat tires from unsuspecting nails left on the roadway or from a large pot hole that has gotten so big it could swallow up your car. I have also seen broken water mains that have flooded streets so badly that you could go swimming in them and for whatever reason the city always takes their sweet time getting out there to fix them.

60. NAKED PEOPLE

I have seen people at their very worst while drunk or on drugs walking butt naked down the street like they are headed to Walmart to do some shopping and are upset with me for stopping them and attempting to put them safely away into my patrol car before the general public has to see them. You especially never forget the hefty ones (obese people) that you wish still had their clothes on and you really did not want to fight with them or roll around on the ground attempting to handcuff them.

61. THIS GUY TASTES FAMILIAR

It amazes me how creative people can get when they are running on foot from the police and they have no place to hide or it appears that way. My police canine has found suspects hiding inside fifty five gallon garbage cans, drainage pipes, under houses, on top of houses, attics, trees, in a pile of leaves, bushes, inside a pile of abandoned old tires, abandoned buildings, homes, inside cars/underneath cars, and out in the woods. The list goes on and on!! The crooks do not realize police dogs use their noses more than they use their eyes and once trained, the dogs pick up very quickly on the odor of the bad guy wherever they hide! Believe it or not my police dog even found the same suspect twice during two totally different criminal episodes! Think about how large the city of Houston is and the odds of finding the same person twice? I could not help but wonder if my police dog remembered how the bad guy tasted from the first bite and then say, "hey this guy tastes familiar during the second bite".

62.   WHAT ELSE COULD GO WRONG?

They had an actor on the ground (suspect running on foot) in the north shepherd station area and officers requested a K-9 unit to search a not so nice apartment complex for a suspect who had assaulted a family member. I arrive on scene with my canine partner and the officers tell me that they had already been chasing this guy who can run like a deer around the complex and had lost him twice. They also tell me that several angry family members (some related to the suspect and some related to the victim) are out walking the complex looking for the suspect as well and they wanted to find him first to kick the guys ass before he goes to jail. I start searching the complex with the dog and we find the guy hiding behind an apartment patio that has a small wooden fence around it. Two other officers and I are standing in a breezeway yelling at the suspect to surrender, but he does not come out. While we are doing this, I see two very large pit bulls located maybe fifty feet away from us, who are jumping up and down inside another small apartment patio and they are pissed off because we are yelling at the guy and my police canine is barking at the suspect.

Now the angry mob of approximately ten to fifteen people who had been searching for the suspect, starts hearing us and knows that we have located this guy. So now things are really heating up around us and the suspect jumps on top of the four feet wooden fence looking around like he is going to run again. What else could possibly go wrong? Well, one of the police officers started taking steps backwards (unknowingly towards me and the dog) to distance himself away from the suspect who is standing on the wooden fence and the police canine accidentally bites the police officer after he stepped on the dogs front right paw. I immediately pull the dog off the officers left arm to focus again on the suspect and the injured officer runs away from the scene holding his injured arm. The other police officer with me grabs the suspect and puts him on the ground to handcuff him. I look to my left and see the angry mob running towards us in the breezeway. I look to my right and see one of the large pit bulls jump over the wooden patio fence and is charging us at full speed. I take my gun out and fire one shot at the dog as he lunges towards us. My bullet strikes the ground and misses the dog, but he runs off scared in the opposite direction. I then turn around to my left looking for the angry mob and they have all scattered from the sound of the gun shot. I guess they figured theses crazy cops are out here shooting at folks and ran for their lives!

63.   HIGH WATER ESCAPE

Some bad guys take extreme measures to escape from being arrested and do very unusual things that normal folks would never even consider. I was once requested to check-by with some westside units that were attempting to arrest a suspect who was involved in an F.S.G.I. (fail to stop and give information) accident and he also had warrants out for his arrest. The suspect abandoned his car at the scene (along with his wallet and driver license) and then fled on foot away from the accident. He then decided to jump into a nearby creek and float downstream to make his final getaway. The primary unit requested a K-9 unit to check by and I was immediately thinking to myself we do not practice or train for high water rescues and/or captures.

I get there to obtain all the details of the incident and description of the suspect. We come up with a plan to follow this guy as he floats downstream by use of a police helicopter and a golf cart that we loaded my canine partner into just waiting for the right opportunity to take some type of action. We followed this guy literally for almost two hours as he continued to float downstream and avoid detection. The guy finally gets tired of being cold and wet and swims closer to the creek bank where he is observed by police still in the water sitting up on a tree log. Myself and my police dog sneak up on the suspect very quietly and I quickly deploy the canine as the suspect attempts to get away again. The canine grabs the suspect by the leg before he could jump back into the creek and he is taken into custody. That guy had a shocked look on his face and could not believe that we had found him after his failed escape. He looked like a wet rat when he was finally placed in the back of the police car and transported to jail.

64. I'M A WRECKER DRIVER

Some calls stick in your mind more than others because of the fear and violence the victim is exposed to during the incident. One such call involved a pregnant female who was robbed at gun point and her vehicle was stolen. The female was walking alone late at night in a parking lot at an apartment complex where she was abducted, raped, and forced to drive to an ATM to withdraw money. Later that evening, she was released by the suspect who used her stolen car for some joy riding and/or additional crimes. Early the next morning around 5:00 a.m. the suspect returned to the same apartment complex driving the victim's car and she called the police after spotting him. Upon arrival to the scene the primary unit sees the suspect driving the stolen vehicle and the suspect attempts to run away on foot. Several patrol units set up a perimeter in the neighborhood and call for a K-9 unit. When I arrive on the scene, we obtain a brief description of the wanted suspect and deploy immediately going yard to yard searching for the bad guy. Upon entering a fenced in backyard my canine partner pulls me toward some large bushes on the corner of the lot where the suspect is attempting to hide on the ground and canine contact is made. We pull the suspect out of the bushes and I am calling via police two-way radio that we have located the suspect. About that time an unknown guy comes running up in plain clothes with some type of ID around his neck and he jumps on top of the suspect who is still on the ground. I asked the guy if he is a police officer and he respond, "I'm a wrecker driver." Immediately, I tell the guy thanks for the help dummy, but to get the heck off my suspect and away from my scene. Other uniformed police officers arrive shortly afterwards in the backyard and take the guy into custody.

65. KARMA

Another similar incident happened in south Houston where a nine-month pregnant female was robbed at gun point by a violent suspect who pointed the gun at her stomach and requested the keys to her car. A short time later officers spot the stolen car being driven by the guy and after a high-speed chase the armed suspect runs off on foot into a neighborhood. Officers set up a perimeter and call for a K-9 unit. We arrive on scene and obtain a brief description of the suspect. I deploy my canine partner and start searching the neighborhood going yard to yard. We somehow get separated from the other officers and start searching the back of a residence that has a large garage built on the south side of the property away from the house. My canine partner starts pulling me towards the right side of the garage and I can now see the suspect who is attempting to hide/conceal himself underneath some bushes located next to the building. I give the suspect verbal commands to come out and surrender, but he does not comply with my orders. I send the police canine and contact is made on one of the legs of the armed suspect. The guy stands up with the canine attached to his leg and I can see a gun tucked in his front right waist band. The suspect refuses to drop his weapon and/or follow my verbal commands, but he is screaming in pain since the police canine is not letting go and still has a firm hold on him. I advise the other police officers of my location via police two-way radio and request back-up immediately.

Officers arrive very quickly in the backyard and take the suspect into custody without further incident. Talk about having a bad day. The bad guy not only got captured (bit) by a police dog, but he had been hiding on the ground under some bushes where a large bed of fire ants was located and he had multiple ant bites all over his entire body. Suspects be advised that "Karma" will get you if you mess with or harm pregnant females. Too bad I did not have a police canine named "Karma!"

66. HOUSE FIRE

I got a call once about an arson suspect that had set his house on fire and later fled the scene on foot butt naked. Upon arrival to the scene, I talk to the firefighters who tell me the guy apparently had some mental issues and set his house on fire after his elderly parents had requested him to move out of the location. The suspect got mad about the situation and decided to burn down the house for some payback. The first firefighter through the door tells me that he saw the suspect who was sitting in a chair butt naked in the middle of the room holding a machete and the house was on fire all around him. The firemen immediately exit from the house since the suspect was armed and appeared to be crazy. When I got there, the firemen do not know if the suspect is still in the house, but one of the neighbors advised that he saw the suspect flee the location on foot.

My canine partner and I go right to work going yard to yard searching for the butt naked crazy guy armed with a machete. About three to four houses down the street, my canine indicates around a ten-foot wooden fence and I peer through the slats to see the suspect squatting down attempting to hide behind a house. I advise the patrol units via police two-way radio of the suspects location and we all run over to his location before he could escape. The patrol officers then take the crazy guy into custody without incident and transport him to the hospital for a mental health evaluation.

67. SURPRISE IN THE STORAGE CONTAINER

I once checked by with some northeast units regarding a suspect who had a road rage incident with some ladies in another car and then decided to pull a gun on them for an attempted robbery. The police were called to the scene to investigate and the suspect was spotted in the area. A foot chase ensues, and the suspect was lost by the officers somewhere inside a neighborhood. The patrol units set up a perimeter around the area and call for a K-9 unit. Upon arrival to the scene I get a brief description of the suspect and we go right to work searching for him in the area. I have just got started searching with my police canine and another unit comes on the police two-way radio saying an elderly neighbor reported possibly seeing someone crawl underneath their house. So, off we go to the new location which is almost a mile away from where we started, and I am hoping the suspect will be underneath this neighbor's house. I get there and walk the police canine around the property and get no type of indication at all. The patrol officers start using their flashlights looking underneath the house and the suspect is not there. I am a little bit angry over the false lead which was a big waste of time and I walk all the way back to the original location where we first started our investigation.

I put the police canine back into search mode and we start searching for the suspect again going yard to yard. We come up to a large metal storage container that is located behind one of the houses. This thing is huge and is sealed from top to bottom except for a small side door that is unlocked. I walk the police dog completely around the structure and he is giving me a slight indication. I open the door and pause for a second looking in to see what is inside this metal box, but it is pitch dark. I use my flashlight to light up the location and see nothing but piles and piles of miscellaneous junk. My police dog is starting to get more excited like something is in there and all kinds of things are going thru my head like could the suspect be hiding in here and possible still armed or could it just be a wild critter like a raccoon or possum. I am also thinking that I should have gotten on the police two-way radio and told someone of my location because nobody knows where I am in case things go south. All I can do is trust my police dog and continue following him with my flashlight as he walks thru this dark obscured structure and hope that he can locate the suspect.

I lose sight of the dog in a dark corner and hear a bunch of noise like miscellaneous things being thrown around during a fight. I move closer and light up the area with my flashlight quick enough to see my police dog grab one of the suspects legs. The suspect somehow pry opens a piece of old rusted sheet metal with his bare hands and crawls out a small hole in the metal box container. The dog is still attached to his leg as they both disappear outside of the metal box. I'm now frantically looking for the side door that I had originally walked through to enter the structure and run outside to assist my four-legged partner who is doing all he can to hold on to the fleeing suspect. Once outside I quickly get on the police two-way radio and request back-up immediately. My canine partner and I are still in a brief struggle with the suspect as our help arrives. The suspect is taken into custody without serious injury besides the canine contact to his leg and an ambulance is called to the scene to provide minor first-aid to him before he is transported to jail. Note to self, always advise the dispatcher of your location, and wait for back-up before going into a structure all alone! We were fortunate that luck was on our side that day and the bad guy was captured.

68.   CHEATING DEATH

When things go bad on a call and something happens to your four-legged partner like a serious injury it can haunt you for the rest of your life. It happened twice to one of my canine partners during routine calls for service and it scared the crap out of me. During the first incident we were looking for two wanted suspects on an abandoned golf course and it was a hot and humid day in Houston. I put my canine partner on the ground and start searching for the bad guys along with another K-9 Team. After about an hour my canine partner finds one of the suspects hiding in some bushes and he is taken into custody. I place my canine back into the air-conditioned police car and give him some water. The second K-9 team continues to search the area looking for the other wanted suspect but must stop their search because of the extreme heat.

The second K-9 officer asks me about twenty to thirty minutes later if I can re-deploy my police dog because he felt the other suspect was somewhere nearby in the area. I cautiously agree to put my dog back into search mode and off we go again tracking the bad guy. We reach a tall grassy knoll on the golf course and can see the second suspect running about four hundred yards away towards a tree line. We keep pushing the dog harder to lead us to the bad guy, but by the time we reach his last known location we are all exhausted and my police dog is showing serious signs of heat exhaustion/stroke. A police helicopter hears about our situation and drops cold bottles of water for the dog, but he is too far gone to be able to drink and needs to be taken to a veterinarian for emergency treatment. The police canine cannot walk on his own and my police car is too far away to safely carry him. The police helicopter makes an emergency landing and picks up the dog at our location and he is quickly transported to the city veterinarian for treatment. The canine is kept overnight at the veterinarian clinic and he makes a full recovery. The second suspect that we were tracking was later found and arrested by patrol officers in a nearby trailer park wearing only his boxer shorts. Both suspects were criminally charged with burglary and taken to jail. The relentless team effort/pursuit put forth in this case involving the Patrol division, K-9 detail, and the Helicopter division resulted in the arrest of two wanted suspects which ended their brief crime spree.

69. CHEATING DEATH (PART 2)

The second incident happened when we were tracking a robbery suspect in the woods during the summertime. After about an hour the suspect was located, my dog started showing signs of heat exhaustion/stroke again and could not walk on his own. I carried the dog back to my police car where he was placed in the air conditioning and attempted to give him water, but he would not drink. I immediately took him to the city veterinarian, and he was once again treated for heat exhaustion/stroke. My canine partner luckily made another full recovery and worked for a total of seven years before getting to retire and enjoy the rest of his life with his family at home!

70. FAMILY JEWELS

Have you ever seen the meme picture posted on social media by K9 Life of the police canine that is staring out the window of a car while it's driving down the street and in the caption it says, "Sometimes I wonder if bad guys are thinking about me too." I laughed so hard after seeing that because I know for a fact that any criminal that has ever been taken down by a police canine is probably still having nightmares about their little encounter and has the scars and/or puncture wounds to prove it!! One of the police dogs assigned to me had an unusually strong bite and even popped three of my son's basketballs in his mouth. I did not like putting him on bad guys because I knew how much damage would be done and they would be taking a trip to the hospital prior to going to jail. In one call, we checked by with some North Shepherd patrol officers that had been dispatched to an armed robbery and the two suspects involved even fired a shot at a security guard who attempted to stop them. The suspects fled into the woods located behind the business and the patrol officers set up a perimeter quickly around the area where they were last seen. K-9 is dispatched to the location and we hit the ground running looking for the bad guys. My canine partner is pulling me through a field towards the two suspects that were attempting to hide/conceal themselves by lying down flat on their stomachs in the brush of the tree line approximately four hundred yards from where we started. I guess they were confident that we would not find them because they did not move until we were right up on them. All of a sudden, I see them jump up to run as we approach them, and I release my canine to give chase. The police dog immediately takes down one of the suspects and I tackle the other bad guy, so he does not get away. Back up arrives and both suspects are taken into custody. We call an ambulance to the scene to provide first-aid to the suspect that got bit by the police canine and they tell me he needs to go to the hospital for treatment. I ask them how bad are his injuries? They tell me the police canine bit him in the family jewels and one of his testicles had been bitten off hanging only by threads out of his man sack. We usually need to look at the damage done by the police canine to document their injuries, but I passed on that one!

71. NEVER LOSE A BATTLE

In the K-9 detail you are taught that your canine should never lose a battle and sometimes it requires you to step in to assist your four-legged partner in a fight. Remember that we track/search for very violent criminals and most are wanted for committing serious felony crimes. These criminals do not want to go to jail and/or go back to prison and will do whatever it takes when you are the only thing keeping them from their freedom.

I was never involved in a shooting my entire career in patrol until I transferred to the K-9 detail and was then involved in two OIS (officer involved shooting). One of the suspects was a murder suspect who was killed during the shootout with police and my police dog was used to clear the vehicle by pulling the bad guy completely out of the car who was still armed with a shotgun. The suspect involved in the second police shooting survived his wounds and was given three life sentences in prison for attempted capital murder of three police K-9 handlers. Several other patrol officers and I involved in the first shooting received an award from the Houston Police Department titled "Hostile Engagement Award", which was presented to each of us by the Chief of Police at the time during an awards ceremony at the Police Academy.

Prior to receiving my award that day I had asked if I could walk across the stage with my police canine partner and felt like he deserved just as much recognition as the rest of us, but the higher ups said no! They told me that the Chief of Police at the time was afraid of dogs and would not let me do it. Not all heroes wear capes, some wear dog tags!